American Prophets
of Peace

Also from Westphalia Press
westphaliapress.org

The Idea of the Digital University	Issues in Maritime Cyber Security
Dialogue in the Roman-Greco World	Understanding Art
Treasures of London	Homeopathy
The History of Photography	Fishing the Florida Keys
International or Local Ownership?: Security Sector Development in Post-Independent Kosovo	Iran: Who Is Really In Charge?
	Contracting, Logistics, Reverse Logistics: The Project, Program and Portfolio Approach
Baronial Bedrooms	
Making Trouble for Muslims	The Thomas Starr King Dispute
Material History and Ritual Objects	Springfield: The Novel
Lankes, His Woodcut Bookplates	Lariats and Lassos
Opportunity and Horatio Alger	Mr. Garfield of Ohio
The Role of Theory in Policy Analysis	The Wisdom of Thomas Starr King
Bookplates of the Kings	The French Foreign Legion
Non Profit Organizations and Disaster	War in Syria
Freemasonry in Old Buffalo	Naturism Comes to the United States
The Idea of Neoliberalism: The Emperor Has Threadbare Contemporary Clothes	Growing Inequality: Bridging Complex Systems, Population Health and Health Disparities
Social Satire and the Modern Novel	
The Essence of Harvard	Designing, Adapting, Strategizing in Online Education
Ukraine vs. Russia: Revolution, Democracy and War: Selected Articles and Blogs, 2010-2016	Gunboat and Gun-runner
	Pacific Hurtgen: The American Army in Northern Luzon, 1945
A Definitive Commentary on Bookplates	
James Martineau and Rebuilding Theology	Natural Gas as an Instrument of Russian State Power
A Strategy for Implementing the Reconciliation Process	World Food Policy
	New Frontiers in Criminology
Gilded Play	Feeding the Global South

American Prophets of Peace

Souvenir of the National Arbitration and
Peace Congress
New York
April 1907

National Arbitration and Peace Congress

WESTPHALIA PRESS
An imprint of Policy Studies Organization

American Prophets of Peace: Souvenir of the National Arbitration and Peace Congress, New York, April 1907
All Rights Reserved © 2017 by Policy Studies Organization

Westphalia Press
An imprint of Policy Studies Organization
1527 New Hampshire Ave., NW
Washington, D.C. 20036
info@ipsonet.org

ISBN-13: 978-1-63391-586-2
ISBN-10: 1-63391-586-7

Cover design by Jeffrey Barnes:
jbarnes.design

Daniel Gutierrez-Sandoval, Executive Director
PSO and Westphalia Press

Updated material and comments on this edition
can be found at the Westphalia Press website:
www.westphaliapress.org

American Prophets of Peace

SOUVENIR OF THE NATIONAL
ARBITRATION AND PEACE CON-
GRESS, NEW YORK, APRIL, 1907

AMERICAN PROPHETS OF PEACE

SOUVENIR OF THE
NATIONAL ARBITRATION AND PEACE CONGRESS
NEW YORK, APRIL, 1907

The Peace Congresses

The first Peace Society in America, or in the world, was founded in New York, by David Low Dodge and his associates, in August, 1815. The Massachusetts Peace Society, which owed its initiative to Noah Worcester, was organized in Dr. Channing's study, in Boston, in the Christmas week of the same year. The London Society was organized the next year; and, from that time on, Peace Societies multiplied. But almost a generation passed before the inauguration of Peace Congresses. The first International Peace Congress was held in London in 1843. It was the thought of the English philanthropist, Joseph Sturge, the friend of Garrison and Whittier and other American anti-slavery leaders, and was first broached by him in Boston in 1841 to members of the American Peace Society. Our society warmly indorsed it and commended it to the English society, and through the co-operation of the two the memorable London Congress was brought about. It was almost exclusively a British and American Congress, 294 of the 337 delegates being from Great Britain, 37 from America, and 6 from the continent of Europe. Perhaps the most important practical proposition considered at this first Congress was that of Judge William Jay, of New York, president of the American Peace Society during the decade in which the historic Peace Congresses in Europe in the middle of the last century occurred, that an arbitration clause should be embodied in all future commercial treaties between the great powers. At the four subsequent Congresses the American representatives stood pre-eminently for the demand for a Congress of Nations, which should develop and codify international law and create an International Tribunal; and this constructive program, which our own day at last is seeing realized, was popularly spoken of in Europe throughout the decade as "the American plan." It was an American, Elihu Burritt, who was the chief inspiring and shaping force for the Brussels Congress in 1848, followed by the great Congresses of Paris, Frankfort, and London, in 1849, 1850, and 1851. At both Paris and Frankfort there were more than twenty American delegates, at London more than sixty. The Paris Congress, over which Victor Hugo presided, and the London Congress, held in the year of the first International Exposition, and having more than a thousand delegates from England alone, were great and impressive gatherings, and in them the peace movement in the last century reached its highest point. They were followed by two important British Congresses, at Manchester and Edinburgh; and then came the Crimean War and the other great wars of that period, and there was a long interregnum.

The first of the present series of International Peace Congresses was held at Paris in 1889, the year of the Paris Exposition. Frederic Passy was its president, and the number of delegates in attendance was almost the same as at the first London Congress in 1843. The second Congress met the next year in London, Hon. David Dudley Field, of New York, serving as its president. The subsequent Congresses have been held at Rome, Berne, Chicago (in 1893), Antwerp, Buda-Pest, Hamburg, Paris, Glasgow, Monaco, Rouen, Boston, Lucerne, and Milan. Of all these International Congresses, that in Boston in 1904 had the largest attendance, its impressive feature being a series of great mass meetings for the people. One of its results was an American delegation of over fifty at the Lucerne Congress the following year, a number five times as great as that which has usually attended the Congresses in Europe during these eighteen years. It is earnestly hoped that an American dele gation as large or larger will be present at the Congress this year, which is to meet at Munich in August or September. It is ten years since the last International Congress was held in Germany,—at Hamburg, in 1897; and this occasion should be embraced for a demonstration of American friendship and admiration for the great German nation, to which our scholars owe so great a debt of gratitude and to which so many millions of our people are bound by the close ties of race.

In recent years, the need for regular National Peace Congresses, in addition to the International Congresses, has been making itself everywhere more and more strongly felt. Comparatively few, at best, of the peace workers in any country are able to attend the Congresses in other countries. To many the hindrances of foreign languages and usages are serious. It is important, moreover, to consolidate and organize the peace party in each country, and by National Congresses to influence public opinion. France, which has taken the lead in so many of the important peace movements of the last twenty years, was the first to act in response to this widespread feeling. The first French National Peace Congress was held at Toulouse in 1902; and subsequent Congresses have been held at Nismes, Lille, and Lyons. England was the second to act; and the Congresses at Manchester, Bristol, and Birmingham in the last three years—the present year's Congress will meet in June at Scarborough—have been large and influential, giving new life and better direction to the English peace movement. The agitation for similar action in Germany is now strong; and the inauguration of German National Congresses is likely to result from conferences of the great number of German peace workers who will gather at Munich in August.

It is at this juncture and with this background that the first American National Peace Congress assembles in New York, in April, 1907. But the Congress has also a distinct American background. The Mohonk Arbitration Conferences, which antedate the English and French Peace Congresses, have in great measure, in addition to their other eminent services, performed the function of National Congresses for America for a dozen years. The education and inspiration in right international thought which they have given the country in the critical period when that influence was most imperatively needed are incalculable. America's obligation to the consecrated and prophetic founder of the Mohonk Conferences is profound. That stimulating nursery and school for effort in the great cities of the country will render ever larger service and have ever wider scope as the Peace Congresses multiply with the years; and we do not fail to remember that Mohonk is in the same Empire State as the city in which our first National Peace Congress meets in 1907, the city in which David Low Dodge founded the first Peace Society in 1815.

Above all other preparations for the new epoch and larger activities of the peace movement in America marked by the assembling of our first National Peace Congress has been the steady, increasing influence of our great Prophets of Peace,—from the founders of the republic, most far-sighted and aspiring statesmen of their time, and from David Dodge and Noah Worcester, to the present hour,—whose lofty conceptions and inspired words have gradually leavened the national thought and wrought that mighty revolution in public opinion which makes the United States to-day so potent a factor in the organization of the united world. In this time of larger life and larger hopes we remember with gratitude and reverence the men who laid the foundations of our temple of peace, and who, being dead, yet speak.

THE NATIONAL ARBITRATION AND PEACE CONGRESS

New York, April 14 to 17, 1907.

ANDREW CARNEGIE, *President.*

Vice-Presidents.

Hon. ANDREW D. WHITE,
  Member First Hague Conference.
Hon. SETH LOW,
  Member First Hague Conference.
Judge GEORGE GRAY,
  Member Hague Permanent Court.
ALBERT K. SMILEY,
  Founder Mohonk Arbitration Conference.
Hon. RICHARD BARTHOLDT, M.C.,
  President American Arbitration Group.
ROBERT TREAT PAINE,
  President American Peace Society.
SAMUEL GOMPERS,
  President American Federation of Labor.
JOHN MITCHELL,
  President United Mine Workers of America.
Hon. ALTON B. PARKER,
  President American Bar Association.
Hon. GEORGE B. MCCLELLAN,
  Mayor of New York.
MORRIS K. JESUP,
  President New York Chamber of Commerce.

Hon. CHARLES E. HUGHES,
  Governor of New York State.
Judge DAVID J. BREWER,
  United States Supreme Court.
Hon. GEORGE B. CORTELYOU,
  Secretary of the Treasury.
Hon. WILLIAM H. TAFT,
  Secretary of War.
Hon. CHARLES J. BONAPARTE,
  Attorney-General.
Hon. GEORGE VON L. MEYER,
  Postmaster-General.
Hon. VICTOR H. METCALF,
  Secretary of the Navy.
Hon. JAMES R. GARFIELD,
  Secretary of the Interior.
Hon. JAMES WILSON,
  Secretary of Agriculture.
Hon. OSCAR S. STRAUS,
  Secretary of Commerce and Labor.
Hon. WILLIAM JENNINGS BRYAN.

ROBERT ERSKINE ELY, *Secretary.*
GEORGE FOSTER PEABODY, *Treasurer.*

EXECUTIVE COMMITTEE

Chairman, Prof. SAMUEL T. DUTTON, Teachers' College, Columbia University.

Secretary, ROBERT ERSKINE ELY, Director League for Political Education.

NEW YORK.

HAYNE DAVIS, American Secretary of the International Conciliation.
RALPH M. EASLEY, Chairman Executive Council of National Civic Federation.
HAMILTON HOLT, Managing Editor of *The Independent.*
Prof. GEORGE W. KIRCHWEY, Dean Columbia University Law School.
HENRY M. LEIPZIGER, Supervisor of Lectures, Board of Education.
Rev. FREDERICK LYNCH, Pastor Pilgrim Congregational Church.
MARCUS M. MARKS, Chairman Conciliation Committee, New York Civic Federation.
JOHN E. MILHOLLAND.
Prof. JOHN BASSETT MOORE, Columbia University.
Mrs. FREDERICK NATHAN.
Miss MARY J. PIERSON.
ERNST RICHARD, President German-American Peace Society.

CHARLES SPRAGUE SMITH, Director People's Institute.
Mrs. ANNA GARLIN SPENCER, Society for Ethical Culture.
Mrs. HENRY VILLARD.

OTHER CITIES.

EDWIN D. MEAD, Boston, Chairman Executive Committee International Peace Congress, 1904.
BENJAMIN F. TRUEBLOOD, Boston, Secretary American Peace Society.
MAHLON N. KLINE, Philadelphia.
STANLEY R. YARNALL, Philadelphia.
JAMES B. REYNOLDS, Washington.
WILLIAM CHRISTIE HERRON, Cincinnati, President Arbitration and Peace Society.
Rev. JENKIN LLOYD JONES, Chicago, Pastor All Souls' Church.
Rabbi J. LEONARD LEVY, Pittsburg.
H. C. PHILLIPS, Secretary Mohonk Arbitration Conference,

GENERAL COMMITTEE

Hon. WILLIAM I. BUCHANAN.
Hon. JOHN W. FOSTER.
Hon. SAMUEL W. MCCALL.
Hon. LEVI P. MORTON.
Hon. CORNELIUS N. BLISS.
Hon. GEORGE F. EDMUNDS.
Pres. CHARLES W. ELIOT.
Pres. ARTHUR T. HADLEY.
Pres. WOODROW WILSON.
Pres. J. G. SCHURMAN.
Pres. EDMUND J. JAMES.
Pres. WILLIAM H. P. FAUNCE.
Cardinal GIBBONS.
Archbishop FARLEY.
Bishop JOHN L. SPALDING.
FELIX ADLER.
Rev. E. E. HALE, D.D.
Bishop HENRY C. POTTER.
Bishop WILLIAM LAWRENCE.
Bishop W. N. MCVICKAR.
T. W. HIGGINSON.
JOHN GRAHAM BROOKS.
Bishop HENRY W. WARREN.
Bishop W. F. MALLALIEU.
Mrs. JULIA WARD HOWE.
Miss LILLIAN D. WALD.
Miss JANE ADDAMS.
Mrs. LUCIA AMES MEAD.
Mrs. MAY WRIGHT SEWALL.

Mrs. ISABEL C. BARROWS.
Rev. LYMAN ABBOTT, D.D.
Rev. C. H. PARKHURST, D.D.
Rev. C. E. JEFFERSON, D.D.
Rev. PHILIP S. MOXOM, D.D.
Rev. RUSSELL H. CONWELL, D.D.
Rev. THOMAS R. SLICER.
Rabbi EMIL G. HIRSCH.
Rabbi JOSEPH SILVERMAN.
EDWIN GINN.
A. B. HEPBURN.
R. FULTON CUTTING.
CLEVELAND H. DODGE.
ELGIN R. L. GOULD.
JOHN CROSBY BROWN.
JOHN B. GARRETT.
JOSHUA L. BAILY.
WILLIAM H. MAXWELL.
Dean JAMES E. RUSSELL.
WILLIAM DEAN HOWELLS.
Major-Gen. F. D. GRANT.
Gen. JAMES GRANT WILSON.
BOOKER T. WASHINGTON.
Rev. L. T. CHAMBERLAIN, D.D.
Rev. CHARLES F. DOLE.
SAMUEL BOWLES.
GEORGE HAVEN PUTNAM.
Pres. M. CAREY THOMAS.
Pres. L. CLARK SEELYE.

RAYMOND L. BRIDGMAN.
ALFRED H. LOVE.
CLINTON ROGERS WOODRUFF.
Hon. WILLIAM N. ASHMAN.
Pres. DAVID STARR JORDAN.
Pres. CARROLL D. WRIGHT.
Pres. ISAAC SHARPLESS.
Pres. JAMES B. ANGELL.
Prof. ELBERT RUSSELL.
Prof. WILLIAM JAMES.
Prof. FRANCIS G. PEABODY.
Prof. HENRY VAN DYKE.
Prof. JOHN BATES CLARK.
Prof. BLISS PERRY.
Hon. ROBERT F. BROUSSARD.
Hon. GEORGE W. TAYLOR.
Hon. JAMES L. SLAYDEN.
Hon. R. O. MOON.
Hon. A. J. MONTAGUE.
Hon. G. W. NORRIS.
Hon. W. A. RODENBURG.
Dean HENRY WADE ROGERS.
HERBERT WELSH.
Hon. SAMUEL R. THAYER.
Rev. JOSIAH STRONG.
Hon. GEORGE F. SEWARD.
SAMUEL B. CAPEN.
MOORFIELD STOREY.

RECEPTION COMMITTEE

Mrs. CHARLES E. HUGHES, *Chairman.*
Mrs. ANDREW CARNEGIE,
Mrs. GEORGE B. MCCLELLAN, } *Vice-Chairmen.*
Miss ADELE M. FIELDE, *Secretary.*

Mrs. ROBERT ABBE.
Mrs. A. A. ANDERSON.
Mrs. C. GRISWOLD BOURNE.
Mrs. HAROLD BROWN.
Mrs. HERMAN C. BUMPUS.
Mrs. NICHOLAS MURRAY BUTLER.
Miss MARY R. CALLENDER.
Mrs. WILLIAM A. CAULDWELL.
Mrs. WILLIAM G. CHOATE.
Mrs. HENRY CLARKE COE.
Mrs. WALTER DAMROSCH.
Miss CAROLINE DE FOREST.
Miss JEANIE B. DUNCAN.
Mrs. SAMUEL T. DUTTON.
Mrs. RICHARD L. EDWARDS.
Mrs. ROBERT ERSKINE ELY.
Mrs. A. LEO EVERETT.
Mrs. STUYVESANT FISH.
Mrs. RICHARD WATSON GILDER.
Mrs. JOHN CLINTON GRAY.
Mrs. BEN ALI HAGGIN.
Mrs. WILLIAM PIERSON HAMILTON.
Mrs. J. BORDEN HARRIMAN.
Mrs. ESTHER HERRMAN.

Mrs. L. EMMET HOLT.
Mrs. ROBERT UNDERWOOD JOHNSON.
Miss BEATRIX JONES.
Mrs. HOWARD MANSFIELD.
Mrs. JOHN E. MILHOLLAND.
Miss URSULA J. MORGAN.
Mrs. BAXTER MORTON.
Mrs. WILLIAM A. PERRY.
Mrs. GEORGE PLACE.
Mrs. JOHN D. PRINCE.
Mrs. N. THAYER ROBB.
Mrs. HILBOURNE L. ROOSEVELT.
Mrs. J. WEST ROOSEVELT.
Mrs. HERBERT L. SATTERLEE.
Mrs. WILLIAM JAY SCHIEFFELIN.
Mrs. VICTOR SORCHON.
Mrs. LORILLARD SPENCER.
Mrs. JAMES SPEYER.
Mrs. CHARLES CHAUNCEY STILLMAN.
Miss MARY FULLER STURGES.
Mrs. HENRY VILLARD.
Mrs. EGERTON LEIGH WINTHROP, Jr.
Mrs. J. A. H. WORTHINGTON.

AMERICAN PROPHETS OF PEACE

GEORGE WASHINGTON

Observe good faith and justice toward all nations. Cultivate peace and harmony with all. Religion and morality enjoin this conduct; and can it be that good policy does not equally enjoin it? It will be worthy of a free, enlightened and, at no distant period, a great nation to give to mankind the magnanimous and too novel example of a people always guided by an exalted justice and benevolence.

Overgrown military establishments are, under any form of government, inauspicious to liberty, and are to be regarded as particularly hostile to republican liberty.

My first wish is to see this plague to mankind [war] banished from the earth, and the sons and daughters of this world employed in more pleasing and innocent amusements than in preparing implements and exercising them for the destruction of mankind.

My first wish is—although it is against the profession of arms, and would clip the wings of some of your young soldiers who are soaring after glory—to see the whole world in peace, and the inhabitants of it as one band of brothers striving who should contribute most to the happiness of mankind.

It is time for the age of knight-errantry and mad heroism to be at an end. Your young military men, who want to reap the harvest of laurels, do not care, I suppose, how many seeds of war are sown; but for the sake of humanity it is devoutly to be wished that the manly employment of agriculture and the humanizing benefits of commerce would supersede the waste of war and the rage of conquest.

I shall never so far divest myself of the feelings of a man interested in the happiness of his fellow-men as to wish my country's prosperity might be built on the ruins of that of other nations.

It would be wise, by timely provisions, to guard against those acts of our own citizens which might tend to disturb peace with other nations, and to put ourselves in a condition to give that satisfaction to foreign nations which we may sometimes have occasion to require of them. I particularly recommend to your consideration the means of preventing those aggressions by our citizens on the territory of other nations, and other infractions of the law of nations, which, furnishing just subject of complaint, might endanger our peace with them.

Peace with all the world is my sincere wish. I am sure it is our true policy.
—*Washington*.

BENJAMIN FRANKLIN

I hope that mankind will at length, as they call themselves reasonable creatures, have reason and sense enough to settle their differences without cutting throats; for, in my opinion, *there never was a good war or a bad peace*. What vast additions to the conveniences and comforts of living might mankind have acquired, if the money spent in wars had been employed in works of public utility! What an extension of agriculture, even to the tops of our mountains; what rivers rendered navigable or joined by canals; what bridges, aqueducts, new roads, and other public works, edifices, and improvements, rendering England a complete paradise, might have been obtained by spending those millions in doing good which in the last war have been spent in doing mischief, in bringing misery into thousands of families, and destroying the lives of so many thousands of working people, who might have performed the useful labor!

All wars are follies, very expensive and very mischievous ones. When will mankind be convinced of this, and agree to settle their differences by arbitration? Were they to do it even by the cast of a die, it would be better than by fighting and destroying each other. . . . Even successful wars at length become misfortunes to those who unjustly commenced them, and who triumphed blindly in their success, not seeing all its consequences.

To me it seems that neither the obtaining or retaining of any trade, how valuable soever, is an object for which men may justly spill each other's blood; that the true and sure means of extending and securing commerce is the goodness and cheapness of commodities; and that the profit of no trade can ever be equal to the expense of compelling it, and of holding it, by fleets and armies. . . . If statesmen had a little more arithmetic or were more accustomed to calculation, wars would be much less frequent.

It is astonishing that the murderous practice of duelling should continue so long in vogue. Formerly, when duels were used to determine lawsuits, from an opinion that Providence would in every instance favor truth and right with victory, they were excusable. At present they decide nothing. A man says something which another tells him is a lie. They fight; but, whichever is killed, the point at dispute remains unsettled. . . . Yet every one of these petty princes makes himself judge in his own cause, condemns the offender without a jury, and undertakes himself to be the executioner.

Justice is as strictly due between neighbor nations as between neighbor citizens. A highwayman is as much a robber when he plunders in a gang as when single, and a nation that makes an unjust war is only a *great gang*.

God grant that not only the love of liberty, but a thorough knowledge of the rights of man, may pervade all the nations of the earth, so that a philosopher may set his foot anywhere on its surface and say, This is my country.—*Franklin*.

THOMAS JEFFERSON

I recoil with horror at the ferociousness of man. Will nations never devise a more rational umpire of differences than force? Are there no means of coercing injustice more gratifying to our nature than a waste of the blood of thousands and the labor of millions of our fellow-creatures? Wonderful has been the progress of human improvement in other lines. Let us hope, then, that the law of nature, which makes virtuous conduct produce benefit and vice loss to the agent in the long run, which has sanctioned the common principle that honesty is the best policy, will in time influence the proceedings of nations as well as individuals, and that we shall at length be sensible that war is an instrument entirely inefficient towards redressing wrong, that it multiplies instead of indemnifying losses.

Had the money which has been spent in the present war in Europe been employed in making roads and conducting canals of navigation and irrigation through the country, not a hovel in the Highlands of Scotland or mountains of Auvergne would have been without a boat at its door, a rill of water in every field, and a road to its market town. ... A war would cost us more than would cut through the isthmus of Darien; and that of Suez might have been opened with what a single year has seen thrown away on the rock of Gibraltar.

I do not believe war the most certain means of enforcing principles. Those peaceable coercions which are in the power of every nation, if undertaken in concert and in time of peace, are more likely to produce the desired effect.

War is not the best engine for us to resort to. Nature has given us one in our commerce which, if properly managed, will be a better instrument for obliging the interested nations of Europe to treat us with justice.

I love peace, and am anxious that we should give the world still another useful lesson, by showing them other modes of punishing injuries than by war, which is as much a punishment to the punisher as to the sufferer.

I abhor war and view it as the greatest scourge of mankind.

Peace has been our principle, peace is our interest, and peace has saved to the world this only plant of free and rational government now existing in it. ... However, therefore, we may have been reproached for pursuing our Quaker system, time will affix the stamp of wisdom on it, and the happiness and prosperity of our citizens will attest its merit. And this, I believe, is the only legitimate object of government, and the first duty of governors, and not the slaughter of men and devastation of the countries placed under their care, in pursuit of a fantastic honor, unallied to virtue or happiness.—*Jefferson*.

SAMUEL ADAMS
Copyright, 1897, by A. W. Elson & Co., Boston

Although the General Court have lately instructed you concerning various matters of very great importance to this Commonwealth, they cannot finish the business of the year until they have transmitted to you a further instruction, which they have long had in contemplation, and which, if their most ardent wish could be obtained, might in its consequences extensively promote the happiness of man.

You are, therefore, hereby instructed and urged to move the United States in Congress assembled to take into their deep and most serious consideration whether any measures can by them be used, through their influence with such of the nations in Europe with whom they are united by treaties of amity or commerce, that national differences may be settled and determined without the necessity of war, in which the world has too long been deluged, to the destruction of human happiness and the disgrace of human reason and government.

If, after the most mature deliberation, it shall appear that no measures can be taken at present on this very interesting subject, it is conceived it would redound much to the honor of the United States that it was attended to by their great Representative in Congress, and be accepted as a testimony of gratitude for most signal favors granted to the said States by Him who is the almighty and most gracious Father and Friend of mankind.

And you are further instructed to move that the foregoing Letter of Instructions be entered on the Journals of Congress, if it may be thought proper, that so it may remain for the inspection of the delegates from this Commonwealth, if necessary, in any future time.—*Letter of Instructions drafted by Samuel Adams for the General Court of Massachusetts, to be forwarded to the Massachusetts delegates in Congress. The history and exact date of the document are unknown. It probably belongs to the period between the close of the Revolution and the adoption of the Constitution.*

One of the three things which, according to Bacon, prepare and dispose a people for war is "a state of soldiery professed." A state of society such as we have reason to anticipate will not so much diminish the influence of the military class as annihilate the whole class, by rendering it useless. When there is no employment and no hope of it for the military class, it can have no continuance. A people highly moral and highly intellectual would not endure the existence of such a distinct class. It would realize the utter incompatibility of the existence of such a class with long-continued peace or with that higher moral and intellectual state to which both nature and duty teach man to aspire. If it be asked how a nation destitute of a military class can be safe from foreign violence and invasion, it may be answered, that the existence of such a class is ever a main inducement to both; for either your military force is weaker than your neighbor's, in which case he is insolent; or it is stronger, in which case you are so; or it is equal, in which case the very uncertainty begets in both a spirit of rivalry, of jealousy, and of war. All experience has shown that a well-appointed militia, defending their own altars and homes, are competent to every purpose of repelling foreign violence and invasion; and a society which should engage in no intrigues, covet no foreign possessions, exemplify in all its conduct a spirit of justice, moderation, and regard for the rights of others, would assume a position the most favorable to predispose its neighbors to adopt toward it a kind and peaceable demeanor. Should it fail, its conduct would be effectual to concentrate around it the affections of its own citizens, and thence produce unanimity and vigor in the use of all the means to which it might be necessitated to resort for the purpose of repelling actual invasion. War is a game ever played for the aggrandizement of the few and for the impoverishment of the many. War-establishments are everywhere scions of despotism; when engrafted on republics, they always begin by determining the best sap to their own branch, and never fail to finish by withering every branch except their own.—*Josiah Quincy.*

DAVID LOW DODGE

The principles of war and the principles of the gospel are as unlike as heaven and hell. The principles of war are terror and force, but the principles of the gospel are mildness and persuasion. Overcome a man by the former, and you subdue only his natural power, but not his spirit. Overcome a man by the latter, and you conquer his spirit and render his natural power harmless. Evil can never be subdued by evil. It is returning good for evil that overcomes evil effectually. It is, therefore, alone the spirit of the gospel that can preserve liberty and produce a lasting peace. Wars can never cease until the principles and spirit of war are abolished.

Mankind have been making the experiment with war for ages to secure liberty and a lasting peace; or, rather, they have ostensibly held out these objects as a cover to their lusts and passions. And what has been the result? Generally the loss of liberty, the overturning of empires, the destruction of human happiness, and the drenching of the earth with the blood of man. In most other pursuits mankind generally gain wisdom by experience; but the experiment of war has not been undertaken to acquire wisdom. It has, in fact, been undertaken and perpetrated for ages to gratify the corrupt desires of men. Is it not important that every one naming the name of Christ should bear open testimony against the spirit and practice of war and exhibit the spirit and temper of the gospel before the world that lies in wickedness, and let their lights shine before men? But what can the men of the world think of such Christians as are daily praying that wars may cease to the ends of the earth, while they have done nothing and are doing nothing to counteract its destructive tendency? It is contrary to fact that war is calculated to preserve liberty and secure a lasting peace; for it has done little else but destroy liberty and peace and make the earth groan under the weight of its terror and distress. It is reserved alone for the triumph of the gospel to produce peace on earth and good will to men.—*From Dodge's "War Inconsistent with the Religion of Jesus Christ."*

NOAH WORCESTER

We regard with horror the custom of the ancient heathen in offering their children in sacrifice to idols. We are shocked with the customs of the Hindoos, in prostrating themselves before the car of an idol to be crushed to death, in burning women alive on the funeral piles of their husbands, in offering a monthly sacrifice by casting living children into the Ganges to be drowned. We read with astonishment of the sacrifices made in the Papal crusades and in the Mahometan and Hindoo pilgrimages. We wonder at the blindness of Christian nations, who have esteemed it right and honorable to buy and sell Africans as property, and reduce them to bondage for life. But that which is fashionable and popular in any country is esteemed right and honorable, whatever may be its nature in the views of men better informed.

But while we look back, with a mixture of wonder, indignation, and pity, on many of the customs of former ages, are we careful to inquire whether some customs which we deem honorable are not the effect of popular delusion, and whether they will not be so regarded by future generations. Is it not a fact that one of the most horrid customs of savage men is now popular in every nation in Christendom? What custom of the most barbarous nations is more repugnant to the feelings of piety, humanity, and justice than that of deciding controversies between nations by the edge of the sword, by powder and ball, or the point of the bayonet? What other savage custom has occasioned half the desolation and misery to the human race? And what but the grossest infatuation could render such a custom popular among rational beings? — *The opening words of Noah Worcester's "Solemn Review of the Custom of War."*

WILLIAM ELLERY CHANNING

It is said that without war to excite and invigorate the human mind, some of its noblest energies will slumber, and its highest qualities—courage, magnanimity, fortitude—will perish. To this I answer that, if war is to be encouraged among nations because it nourishes energy and heroism, on the same principle war in our families and war between neighborhoods, villages, and cities ought to be encouraged; for such contests would equally tend to promote heroic daring and contempt of death. Why shall not different provinces of the same empire annually meet with the weapons of death, to keep alive their courage? We shrink at this suggestion with horror; but why shall contests of nations, rather than of provinces or families, find shelter under this barbarous argument?

If war be a blessing because it awakens energy and courage, then the savage state is peculiarly privileged; for every savage is a soldier, and his whole modes of life tend to form him to invincible resolution. On the same principle, those early periods of society were happy when men were called to contend not only with one another, but with beasts of prey; for to these excitements we owe the heroism of Hercules and Theseus. On the same principle, the feudal ages were more favored than the present; for then every baron was a military chief, every castle frowned defiance, and every vassal was trained to arms. Do we really wish that the earth should again be overrun with monsters or abandoned to savage or feudal violence, in order that heroes may be multiplied? If not, let us cease to vindicate war as affording excitement to energy and courage.

We do not need war to awaken human energy. There is at least equal scope for courage and magnanimity in blessing as in destroying mankind. The condition of the human race offers inexhaustible objects for enterprise and fortitude and magnanimity. In relieving the countless wants and sorrows of the world, in exploring unknown regions, in carrying the arts and virtues of civilization to unimproved communities, in extending the bounds of knowledge, in diffusing the spirit of freedom, and especially in spreading the light and influence of Christianity, how much may be dared, how much endured! Philanthropy invites us to services which demand the most intense and elevated and resolute and adventurous activity. Let it not be imagined that, were nations imbued with the spirit of Christianity, they would slumber in ignoble ease; that, instead of the high-minded murderers who are formed on the present system of war, we should have effeminate and timid slaves. Christian benevolence is as active as it is forbearing. Let it once form the character of a people, and it will attach them to every important interest of society. It will call forth sympathy in behalf of the suffering in every region under heaven. It will give a new extension to the heart, open a wider sphere to enterprise, inspire a courage of exhaustless resource, and prompt to every sacrifice and exposure for the improvement and happiness of the human race. The energy of this principle has been tried and displayed in the fortitude of the martyr and in the patient labors of those who have carried the gospel into the dreary abodes of idolatry. Away, then, with the argument that war is needed as a nursery of heroism! The school of the peaceful Redeemer is infinitely more adapted to teach the nobler as well as the milder virtues which adorn humanity.—*The last words of Channing's First Discourse on War.*

WILLIAM LADD

Believing that the custom of war between Christian nations is barbarous and unnecessary, and being fully assured that the time has at length come when a more cheap, humane, equitable, and Christian method of settling international contests may be obtained, we petition your honorable bodies to take such means as may appear to your wisdom best adapted to this desirable end. The plan which your petitioners would venture to suggest as best adapted to bring about so desirable a consummation is simple and easy to be accomplished. It consists of two distinct parts, either of which may be accomplished without the other; but their practicability and utility would be promoted by the union of both.

1. A Congress of Ambassadors, representing such of the governments of Christendom as shall unite in the measure, for the purpose of digesting a code of international law, to be adopted by the universal consent of the Congress, voting by nations, and binding only on the governments that shall freely adopt it. When this work is carried as far as the circumstances of the times will permit, the Congress may be dissolved, or adjourned *sine die*, to be reassembled when circumstances favorable to a further amelioration of the condition of man may be developed.

2. An International Tribunal, consisting of eminent civilians, appointed by the government of each of the concurring powers, to hold their offices during good behavior, who shall judge all cases brought before them by the mutual consent of any two or more nations, to hold their sessions in any of the countries of the high contracting parties, except in the territory of either of the parties appealing to them for judgment, who shall base their decisions on the above-mentioned code of laws, so far as it is settled, and, when that fails, on the principles of equity, such judgments to be enforced only by the power of public opinion and such other peaceful means as the nations shall adopt by their ambassadors in Congress assembled.

Your petitioners are aware that the progress of such a Congress would be slow, but the results would be the more permanent and valuable. It would begin by adopting those principles which are almost self-evident, and would advance to those which are more doubtful and complicated. Experience has shown that when people once heartily begin to promote a good work, a spirit of mutual concession is generated, which will make crooked things straight, and remove mountains of difficulty, which truth our own country, both under the old confederation and the new constitution, has abundantly exemplified.

It is not long since the world was ruled altogether by the sword, but now "opinion is the queen of the world," and begins to extend her legitimate sway over the nations of the earth. Her power will increase as civilization extends, and the march of civilization is commensurate with the duration of peace and the extent of peace principles. We live in an age when the bare attempt to do that which ought to be done insures success. The speed with which great enterprises are carried to their successful consummation is no more to be measured by the creeping pace of public opinion in bygone ages than the velocity of a railroad car is to be judged by the slow movements of the cumbersome wains of antiquity.

The bare attempt, even if it failed, would be glorious. It would show to the world our desire for the peace and happiness of mankind. But the attempt would not fail if it were persevered in, so as to be distinctly seen and understood by the people of Europe. If only France and Great Britain joined us at first, success would be certain. The work has already begun in England. France will follow. God has destined this country to take the lead in this great enterprise. Let us not be unmindful of our high destiny.—*From the Petition to Congress of the American Peace Society, signed by William Ladd, its President, and the members of its Executive Committee, 1838.*

Few virtues are more universally professed, few are more imperfectly apprehended, and few are more rarely practised, than patriotism. From the time of Absalom to the last electioneering meeting, patriotic professions have been the cheap materials from which demagogues have attempted to construct their fortunes. Counterfeits imply an original. There is such a virtue as patriotism; and it is but a development of that benevolence which springs from moral goodness. To do good unto all men as we have opportunity is an injunction invested with divine authority. Generally our ability to do good is confined to our families, neighbors, and countrymen; and the natural promptings of our hearts lead us to select these in preference to more distant objects, for the subjects of our kind offices. Our benevolence, when directed to our countrymen at large, constitutes patriotism; and its exercise is as much controlled by the laws of morality as when confined to our neighbors or our families. A voice from heaven has forbidden us "to do evil that good may come." The sentiment, "Our country, right or wrong," is as profligate and impious as would be the sentiment, "Our church or our party, right or wrong." It is treason to the cause of civil and religious liberty, of justice and humanity. If it be rebellion against God to violate his laws for the benefit of one individual, however dear to us, not less sinful must it be to commit a similar act for the benefit of any number of individuals. If we may not, in kindness to the highwayman, assist him in robbing and murdering the traveller, what divine law permits us to aid any number of our own countrymen in robbing and murdering other people? He who engages in a defensive war, with a full conviction of its necessity and justice, may be impelled by patriotism, by a benevolent desire to save the lives and property and rights of his countrymen. But if he believes the war to be one of invasion and conquest, and utterly unjust, by taking part in it he assumes its guilt and becomes responsible for its crimes.

WILLIAM JAY

The demagogue who echoes the clamor of the mob gives a very inconclusive proof of his patriotism; while he who, in promoting what he believes to be the public weal, exposes himself to obloquy, may reasonably be regarded as governed by disinterested motives. Patriotism springing from obedience to God and exercised in official station for the national welfare, at the certain and willing loss of popular favor and personal advantage, is perhaps the highest perfection to which this virtue can attain. Much which assumes the name of patriotism, and passes current with the world, is utterly spurious. The patriotism which seeks the public good, in obedience to the divine will, is indeed to be found in camps and senates, but these are not its exclusive nor its favorite haunts. It is chiefly by the patriotism of sincere, faithful Christian men and women, gentle and noiseless as the dew of heaven, prompting innumerable efforts and costly sacrifices of time and money for the welfare of their fellow-countrymen, that our land is clothed with moral verdure and beauty.—*From Judge William Jay's Review of the Causes and Consequences of the Mexican War.*

I know of nothing which better marks the high moral tone of modern history than that the sublime code of international law should have come into form and established its authority over the civilized world within so short a time; for it is now scarcely more than two hundred years since it took its being. In the most polished and splendid age of Greece and Grecian philosophy, piracy was a lawful and even honorable occupation. Nations were considered as natural enemies, and for one people to plunder another by force of arms and to lay their country waste was no moral wrong, any more than for the tiger to devour the lamb. In war, no terms of humanity were binding, and the passions of the parties were mitigated by no constraints of law.

HORACE BUSHNELL

Go now with me to a little French town near Paris, and there you will see in his quiet retreat a silent, thoughtful man bending his ample shoulders and more ample countenance over his table, and recording with a visible earnestness something that deeply concerns the world. This man has no office or authority to make him a lawgiver, other than what belongs to the gifts of his own person—a brilliant mind, enriched by the amplest stores of learning and nerved by the highest principles of moral justice and Christian piety. He is, in fact, a fugitive and an exile from his country, separated from all power but the simple power of truth and reason. But he dares, you will see, to write *De Jure Belli et Pacis*. This is the man who was smuggled out of prison and out of his country, to give law to all the nations of mankind in all future ages. On all seas and on all lands he shall bear sway. In the silence of his study, he stretches forth the sceptre of law over all potentates and peoples, defines their rights, arranges their intercourse, gives them terms of war and terms of peace, which they may not disregard. In the days of battle, too, when kings and kingdoms are thundering in the shock of arms, this same Hugo Grotius shall be there, in all the turmoil of passion and the smoke of ruin, as a presiding throne of law, commanding above the commanders and, when the day is cast, prescribing to the victor terms of mercy and justice, which not even his hatred of the foe, or the exultation of the hour, may dare to transcend.—*From Bushnell's Essay on "The Growth of Law."*

ELIHU BURRITT

The opening of this High Court of Nations must open a new era in the condition and prospects of mankind. A seat for life or for any period on this bench of judges is the highest appointment within the capacity of any nation. . . . Still, it cannot be the place for the ambitious politician, the factious diplomatist, or reckless demagogue. Consequently, we may believe that two profound statesmen or jurists have been appointed by each nation, to represent it in this grand tribunal. Filling the sublimest position to which the suffrage of mankind could raise them, we may presume that they would act under a proper sense of the dignity and responsibility of their vocation. Constituting the highest Court of Appeal this side of the bar of Eternal Justice, they would endeavor, we might hope, to assimilate their decisions, as nearly as possible, to those of unerring Wisdom. Sinking the great disconnected circles of human society into the chain of universal order, they would watch with jealous eye all that could disturb the harmony of nations, the links of which that chain is composed. Such a body, in several senses, would be to the great orbit of humanity what the sun is in the solar system,—if not in the quality of light, at least in that of attraction. A presentiment of union would pervade the nations, and prepare them for a new condition of society. Wherever a question arose between two of them, the thought of war would not occur to either. The note of martial preparations would not be heard along their coasts. The press would not breathe thoughts among the people calculated to stimulate sentiments and presentiments of hostilities. Each party would say to its government, "There is the law; there is the court; there sit the judges! refer the case to their arbitrament, and we will abide by their decision." Instead of the earth being shaken with the thunder of conflicting armies and deluged with blood, to settle a question of right or honor, we should see reported, among other decisions of this Supreme Court of Nations, the case of England *versus* France, Prussia *versus* Denmark, or Mexico *versus* the United States. Thus all these occasions of war, under the old régime of brute force, might be settled as legitimately and satisfactorily as any law case between two sovereign states of the American Union. The Supreme Court of the United States is frequently occupied with a lawsuit between two states; and a case entitled New York *versus* Virginia, or Ohio *versus* Pennsylvania, will often be found on the list of cases presented for trial. A resort to arms never occurs to the inhabitants of either of the litigant states, however grave may be the difference between them. The first result, then, of the erection of this High Court of Nations would be the expulsion of the idea of war from the popular mind of Christendom; and all preparations for war would disappear in like manner. . . . New political affinities have already been created between nations. The community of nations is slowly approximating to the condition of the family circle. Now is the time to organize these social tendencies and national affinities into a fixed system of society. . . . Nations are gravitating into union; not giving up any essential qualities of independence or individuality, but confederating with each other under the attraction of mutual affinities. Then why may we not link these large circles of humanity into one grand system of society, by creating for it a common centre and source of attraction in the establishment of a HIGH COURT OF NATIONS?—*From Elihu Burritt's Address at the International Peace Congress at Brussels in* 1848.

Copyright 1900 by Eugene A. Perry *By Permission of the Perry Pictures Company*

HORACE MANN

If a thousandth part of what has been expended in war and preparing its mighty engines had been devoted to the development of reason and the diffusion of Christian principles, nothing would have been known for centuries past of its terrors, its sufferings, its impoverishment, and its demoralization, but what was learned from history.

Were nations to embark in the cause of education for the redemption of mankind, as they have in that of war for their destruction, the darkest chapters in the history of earthly calamities would soon be brought to a close; but where units have been grudged for education, millions have been lavished for war. While for the one purpose mankind have refused to part with superfluities, for the other they have not only impoverished themselves, but levied burdensome taxes upon posterity. The vast national debts of Europe originated in war, and but for that scourge of mankind they never would have existed. The earth itself could not be pawned for so vast a sum as was expended in war during the twenty-two years preceding the general peace of 1815 by nations calling themselves *Christian*. Were it to be set up at auction, it would not sell for enough to pay its war bills for a single century.

The ministers of the gospel of peace may continue to preach peace, and still find themselves in the midst of war, or of all those passions by which war is engendered, unless the rising generation shall be educated to that strength and sobriety of intellect which shall dispel the insane illusions of martial glory, and unless they shall be trained to the habitual exercise of those sentiments of universal brotherhood for the race, which shall change the common heroism of battle into a horror and an abomination.

How little do many of the popular histories record but the destruction of human life and the misguided energies of men, which have hitherto almost baffled the beneficent intentions of Nature for human happiness! Descriptions of battles, sackings of cities, and the captivity of nations follow each other in an endless succession. The reader sees rulers and legislators engaged not in devising comprehensive plans for universal welfare, but in levying and equipping armies and navies, and extorting taxes to maintain them. Rarely do these records administer any antidote against the inhumanity of the spirit they instil. They exhibit the triumphal return of warriors, to be crowned with honors worthy of a god, while they take the mind wholly away from the carnage of the battlefield, from desolate provinces and a mourning people. It is as though children should be taken to behold from afar the light of a city on fire, and directed to admire the splendor of the conflagration, without a thought of the tumult and terror and death reigning beneath it. Indeed, if the past history of our race is to be much read by children, it should be rewritten; and while it records those events which have contravened all the principles of social policy and violated all the laws of morality and religion, there should be some recognition of the great truth that, among nations as among individuals, the highest welfare of all can only be effected by securing the welfare of each.—*Horace Mann.*

By the kindness of Houghton, Mifflin & Co.

WILLIAM LLOYD GARRISON

My country is the world; my countrymen are all mankind.

We know not where to look for Christianity if not to its founder; and, taking the record of his life and death, of his teaching and example, we can discover nothing which even remotely, under any conceivable circumstances, justifies the use of the sword or rifle on the part of his followers. On the contrary, we find nothing but self-sacrifice, willing martyrdom (if need be), peace and good will, and the prohibition of all retaliatory feelings enjoined upon all who would be his disciples. When he said, "Fear not those who kill the body," he broke every deadly weapon. When he said, "My kingdom is not of this world, else would my servants fight that I should not be delivered to the Jews," he plainly prohibited war in self-defence, and substituted martyrdom therefor. When he said, "Love your enemies," he did not mean, "Kill them if they go too far." When he said, while expiring on the cross, "Father, forgive them, for they know not what they do," he did not treat them as a "herd of buffaloes," but as poor, misguided, and lost men. We believe in his philosophy. We accept his instruction. We are thrilled by his example. We rejoice in his fidelity. . . . In the name of Jesus of Nazareth, who suffered himself to be unresistingly nailed to the cross, we solemnly protest against any of his professed followers resorting to carnal weapons under any pretext or in any extremity whatever.

The history of mankind is crowded with evidences proving that physical coercion is not adapted to moral regeneration; that the sinful dispositions of man can be subdued only by love; that evil can be exterminated from the earth only by goodness; that it is not safe to rely upon an arm of flesh to preserve us from harm; that there is great security in being gentle, harmless, long-suffering, and abundant in mercy; that it is only the meek who shall inherit the earth, for the violent who resort to the sword shall perish with the sword.

War is as capable of moral analysis as slavery, intemperance, licentiousness, or idolatry. It is not an abstraction which admits of doubt or uncertainty, but as tangible as bombs, cannon, mangled corpses, smouldering ruins, desolated towns and villages, rivers of blood. It is substantially the same in all ages, and cannot change its moral features. Nothing is more terribly distinct than its career. It leaves its impress on everything it touches, whether physical, mental, or moral.—*Garrison.*

I was summoned by the voice of God to decide whether I would stand for or against war. I saw that it was a vast system of manslaughter, even in its most excusable form,—unfraternal, savage, and barbarous; anti-Christian, irrational, and full of monstrous evils. I saw that it was based on the assumed rightfulness of resisting evil with evil and overcoming deadly force with deadly force, which Christ both by precept and example unqualifiedly forbade His disciples to do, even toward their worst enemies. He had lain His great regenerative axe at the root of this upas-tree, and it must be destroyed, trunk and branches. I was fully convinced of this, and took my stand accordingly. Beginning where the Son of God did, I left no room for compromise with the least of its rootlets or sprigs. Starting from the divine fundamental principle of pure, universal good will, absolute love, I felt bound to go with that principle wherever it carried me, for all that it dictated, against all that it condemned.—*Adin Ballou.*

ADIN BALLOU

By the kindness of Houghton, Mifflin & Co.

John G. Whittier

Your Waterloo and battles of the Nile and Baltic,—what are they, in sober fact, but gladiatorial murder games on a great scale,—human imitations of bull-fights, at which Satan sits as grand alguazil and master of ceremonies? It is only when a great thought incarnates itself in action, desperately striving to find utterance even in sabre-clash and gun-fire, or when Truth and Freedom, in their mistaken zeal and distrustful of their own powers, put on battle harness, that I can feel any sympathy with merely physical daring. The bull-dog ferocity of a half-intoxicated Anglo-Saxon, pushing his blind way against the converging cannon fire from the shattered walls of Ciudad Rodrigo, commends itself neither to my reason nor my fancy. The brawny butcher-work of men whose wits, like those of Ajax, lie in their sinews, is no realization of my ideal of true courage. My admiration of heroic achievement has found new and better objects. I have learned to appreciate what Milton calls the martyr's "unresistible might of meekness,"— the calm, uncomplaining endurance of those who can bear up against persecution uncheered by sympathy or applause, and, with a full and keen appreciation of the value of all which they are called to sacrifice, confront danger and death in unselfish devotion to duty. Fox, preaching through his prison gates or rebuking Oliver Cromwell in the midst of his soldier court; Henry Vane beneath the axe of the headsman; Mary Dyer on the scaffold at Boston; Luther closing his speech at Worms with the sublime emphasis of his "Here stand I; I cannot otherwise; God help me"; William Penn defending the rights of Englishmen from the bale dock of the Fleet prison; Clarkson climbing the decks of Liverpool slave ships; Howard penetrating to infected dungeons; meek Sisters of Charity breathing contagion in thronged hospitals,—all these, and such as these, now help me to form the loftier ideal of Christian heroism.

Lend, once again, that holy song a tongue,
Which the glad angels of the Advent sung,
Their cradle-anthem for the Saviour's birth,
Glory to God, and peace unto the earth!
Through the mad discord send that calming word
Which wind and wave on wild Genesareth heard,—
Lift in Christ's name his cross against the Sword!

Whittier.

RALPH WALDO EMERSON

War to sane men at the present day begins to look like an epidemic insanity, breaking out here and there like the cholera or influenza, infecting men's brains instead of their bowels. It is the ignorant and childish part of mankind that is the fighting part. To men of a mature spirit, in whom is any knowledge or mental activity, the detail of battle becomes insupportably tedious and revolting. War and peace resolve themselves into a mercury of the state of cultivation. The sympathy with war is a juvenile and temporary state. Not only the moral sentiment, but trade, learning and whatever makes intercourse conspire to put it down. Trade brings men to look each other in the face, and gives the parties the knowledge that these enemies over sea or over the mountain are such men as we; and learning and art, and especially religion, weave ties that make war look like fratricide, as it is. History is the record of the mitigation and decline of war, though the slow decline. For ages the human race has gone on under the tyranny of this first brutish form of their effort to be men, for ages showed so much of the nature of the lower animals, the tiger and the shark. But the eternal germination of the better has unfolded new powers, new instincts. The sublime question has startled one and another happy soul in different quarters of the globe,—Cannot love be, as well as hate? Cannot peace be, as well as war? This thought has now become so distinct as to be a social thought. This having come, much more will follow. Revolutions go not backward. So it is not a great matter how long men refuse to believe the advent of peace: war is on its last legs; and a universal peace is as sure as is the prevalence of civilization over barbarism, of liberal governments over feudal forms. The question for us is only *How soon?*

A lesson which all history teaches wise men is to trust in ideas, and not in circumstances. We have all grown up in the sight of frigates and navy yards, of arsenals and militia. This vast apparatus of artillery, of fleets, of stone bastions and trenches and embankments; this incessant patrolling of sentinels; this waving of national flags; this martial music and endless playing of marches and singing of military and naval songs, seem to us to constitute an imposing actual, which will not yield in centuries to the feeble, deprecatory voices of a handful of friends of peace. Thus always we are daunted by the appearances, not seeing that their whole value lies at bottom in the state of mind. It is really a thought that built this portentous war-establishment, and a thought shall also melt it away. The standing army, the arsenal, the camp and the gibbet do not appertain to man. They only serve as an index to show where man is now; what a bad, ungoverned temper he has; what an ugly neighbor he is; how his affections halt; how low his hope lies. He who loves the bristle of bayonets only sees in their glitter what beforehand he feels in his heart. The least change in the man will change his circumstances. If, for example, he could come to feel that every man was another self with whom he might come to join, as left hand works with right—every degree of the ascendency of this feeling would cause the most striking changes of external things: the tents would be struck; the men-of-war would rot ashore; the arms rust; the cannon would become street-posts. So it must and will be: bayonet and sword must first retreat a little from their ostentatious prominence; then quite hide themselves, as the sheriff's halter does now, inviting the attendance only of relations and friends; and then, lastly, will be transferred to the museums of the curious, as poisoning and torturing tools are at this day.

The cause of peace is not the cause of cowardice. If peace is sought to be defended or preserved for the safety of the luxurious and the timid, it is a sham, and the peace will be base. War is better, and the peace will be broken. If peace is to be maintained, it must be by brave men, who have come up to the same height as the hero, namely, the will to carry their life in their hand, and stake it at any instant for their principle, but who have gone one step beyond the hero, and will not seek another man's life; men who have, by their intellectual insight, or else by their moral elevation, attained such a perception of their own intrinsic worth, that they do not think property or their own body a sufficient good to be saved by such dereliction of principle as treating a man like a sheep. If the rising generation can be provoked to think it unworthy to nestle into every abomination of the past, and shall feel the generous darings of austerity and virtue, then war has a short day.

Whenever we see the doctrine of peace embraced by a nation, we may be assured it will not be one that invites injury; but one, on the contrary, which has a friend in the bottom of the heart of every man, even of the violent and the base; one against which no weapon can prosper; one which is looked upon as the asylum of the human race and has the blessings of mankind.... In this broad America of God and man, where the forest is only now falling, and the green earth opens to the inundation of emigrant men from all quarters of oppression and guilt,—here, where not a family, not a few men, but mankind, shall say what shall be,—here, we ask, Shall it be War, or shall it be Peace?—*From Emerson's Essay on War.*

THE ARSENAL AT SPRINGFIELD.

This is the Arsenal. From floor to ceiling,
   Like a huge organ, rise the burnished arms;
But from their silent pipes no anthem pealing
   Startles the villages with strange alarms.

Ah! what a sound will rise, how wild and dreary,
   When the death-angel touches those swift keys!
What loud lament and dismal Miserere
   Will mingle with their awful symphonies!

I hear even now the infinite fierce chorus,
    The cries of agony, the endless groan,
Which, through the ages that have gone before us,
    In long reverberations reach our own; . . .

The tumult of each sacked and burning village;
    The shout that every prayer for mercy drowns;
The soldiers' revels in the midst of pillage;
    The wail of famine in beleaguered towns;

The bursting shell, the gateway wrenched asunder,
    The rattling musketry, the clashing blade;
And ever and anon, in tones of thunder
    The diapason of the cannonade.

Is it, O man, with such discordant noises,
    With such accursed instruments as these,
Thou drownest Nature's sweet and kindly voices,
    And jarrest the celestial harmonies?

Were half the power that fills the world with terror,
    Were half the wealth bestowed on camps and courts,
Given to redeem the human mind from error,
    There were no need of arsenals or forts:

The warrior's name would be a name abhorred!
    And every nation, that should lift again
Its hand against a brother, on its forehead
    Would wear forevermore the curse of Cain!

Down the dark future, through long generations,
    The echoing sounds grow fainter and then cease;
And like a bell, with solemn, sweet vibrations,
    I hear once more the voice of Christ say, "Peace!"

Peace! and no longer from its brazen portals
    The blast of War's great organ shakes the skies!
But beautiful as songs of the immortals,
    The holy melodies of love arise.

Longfellow.

THE FATHERLAND.

Where is the true man's fatherland?
   Is it where he by chance is born?
   Doth not the yearning spirit scorn
In such scant borders to be spanned?
Oh yes! his fatherland must be
As the blue heaven wide and free!

Is it alone where freedom is,
   Where God is God and man is man?
   Doth he not claim a broader span
For the soul's love of home than this?
Oh yes! his fatherland must be
As the blue heaven wide and free!

Where'er a human heart doth wear
   Joy's myrtle-wreath or sorrow's gyves,
   Where'er a human spirit strives
After a life more true and fair,
There is the true man's birthplace grand,
His is a world-wide fatherland!

Where'er a single slave doth pine,
   Where'er one man may help another,—
   Thank God for such a birthright, brother,—
That spot of earth is thine and mine!
There is the true man's birthplace grand,
His is a world-wide fatherland!   —*Lowell.*

Oliver Wendell Holmes.

A HYMN OF PEACE.

Angel of Peace, thou hast wandered too long!
    Spread thy white wings to the sunshine of love!
Come while our voices are blended in song,—
    Fly to our ark like the storm-beaten dove!
Fly to our ark on the wings of the dove,—
    Speed o'er the far-sounding billows of song,
Crowned with thine olive-leaf garland of love,—
    Angel of Peace, thou hast waited too long!

Joyous we meet, on this altar of thine
    Mingling the gifts we have gathered for thee,
Sweet with the odors of myrtle and pine,
    Breeze of the prairie and breath of the sea,-
Meadow and mountain and forest and sea!
    Sweet is the fragrance of myrtle and pine,
Sweeter the incense we offer to thee,
    Brothers once more round this altar of thine!

Angels of Bethlehem, answer the strain!
    Hark! a new birth-song is filling the sky!—
Loud as the storm-wind that tumbles the main
    Bid the full breath of the organ reply,—
Let the loud tempest of voices reply,—
    Roll its long surge like the earth-shaking main!
Swell the vast song till it mounts to the sky!—
    Angels of Bethlehem, echo the strain!

CHARLES SUMNER

That Future, which filled the lofty vision of sages and bards in Greece and Rome, which was foretold by Prophets and heralded by Evangelists, when man, in Happy Isles, or in a new Paradise, shall confess the loveliness of Peace, may you secure, if not for yourselves, at least for your children! *Believe* that you can do it, and you *can* do it. The true Golden Age is before, not behind. If man has once been driven from Paradise, while an angel with flaming sword forbade his return, there is another Paradise, even on earth, which he may make for himself, by the cultivation of knowledge, religion, and the kindly virtues of life.

Is it said that the age does not demand this work? The robber conqueror of the Past, from fiery sepulchre, demands it; the precious blood of millions unjustly shed in War, crying from the ground, demands it; the heart of the good man demands it; the conscience, even of the soldier, whispers, "Peace!" There are considerations springing from our situation and condition which fervently invite us to take the lead. Here should join the patriotic ardor of the land, the ambition of the statesman, the effort of the scholar, the pervasive influence of the press, the mild persuasion of the sanctuary, the early teaching of the school. Here, in ampler ether and diviner air, are untried fields for exalted triumph, more truly worthy the American name than any snatched from rivers of blood. War is known as the *Last Reason of Kings*. Let it be no reason of our Republic. Let us renounce and throw off forever the yoke of a tyranny most oppressive of all in the world's annals. As those standing on the mountain-top first discern the coming beams of morning, so may we, from the vantage-ground of liberal institutions, first recognize the ascending sun of a new era! Lift high the gates, and let the King of Glory in,—the King of True Glory,—of Peace!

So let us dedicate to Peace our beloved country; and may the blessed consecration be felt in all its parts, everywhere throughout its ample domain! The Temple of Honor shall be enclosed by the Temple of Concord, that it may never more be entered through any portal of War; the horn of Abundance shall overflow at its gates; the angel of Religion shall be the guide over its steps of flashing adamant; while within its happy courts, purged of Violence and Wrong, JUSTICE, returned to the earth from long exile in the skies, with equal scales for nations as for men, shall rear her serene and majestic front; and by her side, greatest of all, CHARITY, sublime in meekness, hoping all and enduring all, shall divinely temper every righteous decree, and with words of infinite cheer inspire to those deeds that cannot vanish away. And the future chief of the Republic, destined to uphold the glories of a new era, unspotted by human blood, shall be first in Peace, first in the hearts of his countrymen.—*From Sumner's "The True Grandeur of Nations."*

PHILLIPS BROOKS

Would you see loyalty, implicit obedience, and the complete acceptance of a law which is supreme? Where will you find them so absolute as in the eager intensity with which the scientist watches the face of Nature to catch the slightest intimation of her will? Would you see magnanimity? Where is it so entire as in the heart of the true merchant who feels the common wealth surrounding his personal fortunes and furnishing at once the sufficient means and the worthy purpose of his becoming rich? Would you see self-surrender? Its noblest specimens have not been on the field of battle where the dying soldier has handed the cup of water to his dying foe. They have been in the lanes and alleys of great cities where quiet and determined men and women have bowed before the facts of human brotherhood and human need, and given the full cups of their entire lives to the parched lips of their poor brethren. We learned during the great war that the heroism of the President might be every whit as great and splendid as the heroism of the General. The enthusiasm of the truth-seeker may be as glowing and unselfish as the enthusiasm which scales the height and captures the citadel with the resistless sword.

There is nothing good or glorious which war has brought forth in human nature which peace may not produce more richly and more permanently. When we cease to think of peace as the negative of war, and think of war as the negative of peace, making war and not peace the exception and interruption of human life, making peace and not war the type and glory of existence, then shall shine forth the higher soldiership of the higher battles. Then the first military spirit and its works shall seem to be but crude struggles after, and rehearsals for, that higher fight, the fight after the eternal facts and their obedience, the fight against the perpetually intrusive lie, which is the richer glory of the riper man. The facts of government, the facts of commerce, the facts of society, the facts of history, the facts of man, the facts of God, in these, in the perception of their glory, in the obedience to their compulsion, shall be the possibility and promise of the soldier statesman, the soldier scientist, the soldier philanthropist, the soldier priest, the soldier man. "The sword is beaten into the ploughshare, the spear into the pruning-hook." "The war-drum throbs no longer, and the battle flags are furled." But it is not that the power of fight has perished: it is that the battle has gone up on to higher ground, and into higher light. The battle is above the clouds.—*From Phillips Brooks's Sermon before the Ancient and Honorable Artillery Company of Boston.*

JOSEPHINE SHAW LOWELL

In ceaseless labor, swift, unhurriedly,
She sped upon her tireless ministries,
Endeavoring the help that shall not hurt;
Seeking to build in every human heart
A temple of justice—that no brother's burden
Should heavier prove through human selfishness.

   . . . Faith than sin is mightier,
And by this faith we live,—that in thy time,
In thine own time, the good shall crush the ill;
The brute within the human shall die down;
And love and justice reign, where hate prevents,—
That love which in pure hearts reveals thine own
And lights the world to righteousness and truth.
Richard Watson Gilder.

Made in the USA
Coppell, TX
18 February 2023